THIS BOOK IS A GIFT TO
the Pittsburg Library
from

Soroptimist
International
of Pittsburg

Frédéric
CHOPIN

TELL ME ABOUT

Frédéric
CHOPIN

by Jacqueline Dineen

Carolrhoda Books, Inc. / Minneapolis

Carolrhoda Books, Inc., c/o The Lerner Publishing Group
241 First Avenue North, Minneapolis, Minnesota 55401 U.S.A.
Website address: www.lernerbooks.com

Library of Congress Cataloging-in-Publication Data

Dineen, Jacqueline.
  Frédéric Chopin / by Jacqueline Dineen.
    p. cm.
  Includes index.
  Summary: A biography of the great Polish-French composer who, when
only fifteen years old, received a diamond ring for playing his own
musical composition for the czar of Russia.
  ISBN 1–57505–248–2 (alk. paper)
  1. Chopin, Frédéric, 1810–1849—Juvenile literature. 2. Composers—
Biography—Juvenile literature. [1. Chopin, Frédéric, 1810–1849.
2. Composers.] I. Title. II. Series: Tell me about (Minneapolis, Minn.)
ML3930.C46D56   1998
786.2'092—dc21   97–10855
[B]

Printed by Graficas Reunidas SA, Spain
Bound in the United States of America
1 2 3 4 5 6 – OS – 03 02 01 00 99 98

One evening in 1818, a little boy sat down at the piano and gave his first public concert. He wore a velvet jacket with a white lace collar. When he was done, people clapped and clapped. His mother asked him what they had liked most. "My collar, Mama," the boy said. The boy was Frédéric Chopin. He did not know that he would become one of the world's greatest composers.

A painting of Frédéric Chopin as a young man

Frédéric Chopin was born in Poland in 1810. He had three sisters. Frédéric's parents taught their children about music when they were very young. By the time Frédéric was eight years old, he was composing music of his own.

The house where Frédéric was born, near Warsaw, Poland

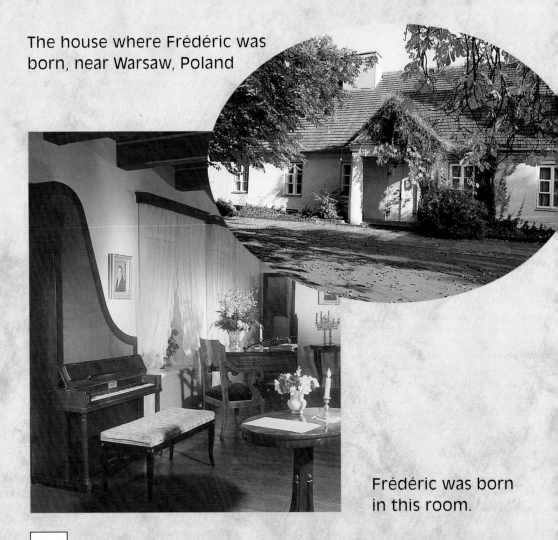

Frédéric was born in this room.

When Frédéric was fifteen years old, he performed for the czar of Russia. He played music he had written himself. The czar enjoyed the performance so much that he gave Frédéric a diamond ring.

Not long after Frédéric visited Russia, the Poles revolted against Czar Nicholas I.

When Frédéric was seventeen, his sister Emilia became ill and died. Frédéric was very sad. He worked hard at his music to get over the loss.

Frédéric wrote many kinds of music, including music for Polish dances. Robert Schumann, a composer, praised Frédéric's music in a newspaper article. Frédéric was becoming famous.

People still like to dance Polish folk dances.

Vienna in Frédéric's time

Schumann liked Frédéric's music.

Frédéric was asked to play in a big concert in the Austrian city of Vienna. The people loved his music. But the next time he played in Vienna, the people were not interested in his music anymore. They wanted to hear waltzes instead.

News reached Vienna that the Poles were fighting the Russians. Frédéric thought he should join the Polish army, but his father said he would not make a good soldier. He said it was Frédéric's duty to write music that would tell people about Poland.

The Russians ruled Poland in Frédéric's time. The Poles fought the Russians for their freedom.

Frédéric met many musicians and artists in Paris.

Frédéric knew his father was right. He went to Paris and worked as a piano teacher for rich people, who became his friends. He didn't have much money but his new friends helped him.

Rich and famous people often asked Frédéric to come to their big houses and play the piano.

Frédéric playing to a Polish prince and his friends

Piano music
written by
Frédéric

Frédéric composing
music in Paris

When he was twenty-five, Frédéric fell in love
with a young woman named Maria Wodzinska.
Her family would not give him permission to
marry her. By this time, Frédéric had become ill.
He coughed blood and was very weak.

Then Frédéric met a famous French writer. She called herself George Sand. At that time, men had much more freedom than women. George didn't like this, so she used a man's name and often wore men's clothing. Frédéric and George went to Majorca, an island near Spain.

George Sand

The island of Majorca in Frédéric's time

They lived together in a small house. At first they were happy, but then the weather became bitterly cold. The cold winds made Frédéric sick again.

A drawing of Frédéric by George Sand

Frédéric and George went to live in France. Frédéric kept on writing music. Sometimes he would perform. Frédéric and George stayed together for nine years, but they argued a lot.

George Sand's house, where Frédéric lived

When Frédéric was thirty-seven, he left George. He was very lonely without her and couldn't work on his music. Then he was asked to give a concert. His health was not good, but he played brilliantly. It was his last concert in Paris.

Frédéric played his last concerts on this grand piano.

In 1848, there was bitter fighting in Paris. Many French people were angry at their king because there was not enough food and they were starving. Frédéric escaped to London. People in London wanted to meet the famous pianist, and they invited him to big parties.

Frédéric needed money so he gave concerts, but the London fog made his health worse.

Frédéric went to London to escape the fighting in Paris.

Frédéric returned to Paris. He wrote to his sister Ludwika, asking her to come and take care of him. Ludwika stayed with Frédéric until he died of tuberculosis in 1849. He was thirty-nine.

People still put flowers on Frédéric's tomb in Paris.

Frédéric spent most of his life in Paris, but he never forgot Poland. Many of his pieces are based on Polish dances and show the spirit of his people. People everywhere still love his music.

Frédéric Chopin's music is often played at concerts.

Important Dates

1810 Frédéric Chopin born in Poland
1818 First public performance
1823 Began music school
1825 Played for Czar Alexander I of Russia
1827 Sister Emilia died
1829 Performed in Vienna
1830 Decided not to be a soldier
1831 Went to Paris
1836 Proposed marriage to Maria Wodzinska
Met George Sand
1838 Went to Majorca
1839 Returned to France
1847 Left George Sand
1848 Gave last concert in Paris
Went to London
Returned to Paris
1849 Frédéric Chopin died

Key Words

composer
a person who writes music

concert
an event where people gather to listen to musicians play

pianist
a person who plays the piano

waltz
a kind of music that can be danced to in a pattern of
one-two-three, *one*-two-three

Index

Acknowledgments

The author and publisher gratefully acknowledge the following for permission to reproduce copyrighted material:
Cover Private Collection, Bridgeman Art Library
Title page Hulton Deutsch
page 5 AKG **page 6** (left) AKG (right) ZEFA **page 7** AKG **page 8** Anna Tully/ Hutchison Library **page 9** (left) Private Collection, Bridgeman Art Library (right) AKG **page 10** AKG London **page 11** Christies, London/Bridgeman Art Library **page 12** AKG **page 13** (top) Hulton Deutsch (bottom) Mary Evans Picture Library **page 14** (top) Mary Evans Picture Library (bottom) Christies, London/Bridgeman Art Library **page 15** Hulton Deutsch **page 16** Erich Lessing/AKG **page 17** Hulton Deutsch **page 18** AKG **page 19** AKG **page 20** Clive Barda, Performing Arts Library **page 21** AKG

About the Author

Jacqueline Dineen began her career as an editor for an educational publisher in London before becoming a children's book writer. She has written more than eighty books on a variety of subjects, including science, history, and geography.